to
struggled to be herself, who wasn't sure who *herself* was, though she had some ideas; who was confused, hurt and felt abandoned by her own thoughts, feelings and desires.

To the little girl who struggled for so many years, and through growing up; from the broken hearts, to the bullying, to the sense of never quite feeling right, in her body, in any space; even in her mind.

To the little girl that never felt like she was smart enough, talented enough, fast enough, pretty enough, enough of *something* enough to ever quite fit in. But to being **wise** enough to create her own world, where *she was **enough***. To having the intuition to turn to something as constructive as writing, rather than something that could have defined her future for her, or ended it before it even started. For having the strength to recognize that she couldn't handle it all on her own, and though she didn't feel like there was anyone she could talk to about daily happenings, she found her own outlet. For never giving up, no matter how many times she wanted to. For trying; always, always trying. For learning as much as she could, of whatever she could.

Lastly, for loving herself enough to, eventually, learn how to **be** herself, fearlessly, shamelessly, and unapologetically while remaining kind and compassionate to others, their difference and their struggles. I know she didn't think she would make it, or didn't know how she would turn out, but she did great. She should be proud of herself; I am of her.

I *also* dedicate this book to those, of all ages, backgrounds; experiences, who struggle day-to-day to be themselves, to *find* themselves; to **express** themselves. I know how hard it can be, I know how hard it **is**, I know how sometimes it's easier to just *give up* and **give in** than it is to give it another fight, but do **not** give up, do **not** give in, you *can* get through this, as grim as your past, present and future may seem, there is a light at the end of the tunnel, there are people waiting to hold your hand; there are people *like* you who will **get** you, *love* you; understand you. I know it doesn't seem like so right now, but It Will Get Better; you just have to hang in there a little bit longer.

Author's Notes

This book is a consolidation of years of private thoughts and secret escapes, of personal victories and untouched observations; some of my darkest of darkness and truest of truth, tucked away safely. It is my desire that anyone who reads this can get a sense of security in knowing that they are not alone in their struggles and to be more compassionate to themselves and others; we all have our struggles, we can all get through them.

I am not a perfect person; I have made mistakes and hurt people; while reading this book, you will see that. I sincerely hope that instead of judging based on the content; you will see it as a testament of the human condition; it's less about what you've been through, and more about what you make of it.

Preface

My name is Leah Slone, I go by Lee, ever since I was a young child, writing has been an outlet, an escape, what I turned to when I needed to get things out but either didn't know how to express myself, or simply couldn't properly articulate what it was I was feeling, or trying to say; so writing was where I went, as a way to, privately, express myself in a judgment free zone, somewhere I could easily tuck away and only take out and share at my *own* wanting.

Some people write as a hobby, some as a career, and they do so out of requirement or for leisure sake; for I, however, writing is more than just what I do, it's who I am. It's the essence of my being; I breathe the words I speak, I speak the words I believe; I believe the words I live by. Writing, the use, placement, value of and emotion behind words, has both figuratively, and literally, saved my life. Words live; words are alive; words give life. 26 little letters create a whole language that shapes and influences an entire people, words command to be appreciated, and respected, yet too often, are not; too often words are misused, abused and, generally, confused.

I've always had the uncanny ability to put thoughts, both of my own and others', into words, even if I couldn't verbally articulate them, or they couldn't; this being said, I have written many pieces *for* others, in an attempt to express and convey what it was they were thinking and/or feeling, often being told that I 'Said it perfectly right.'

Before I get too off on a tangent that is the beauty in words- I'm writing this as a means to make public a part of my life that for so long was nothing but private, hidden away in a small corner of the room, not to be seen, spoken of or known about, a reality within the pages of a folder that no one, outside of myself, even knew existed. A time in my life when words and writing saved my life, gave me purpose, gave me a reason; gave me an escape. It was in this time that I truly learned, began to ***really*** understand and appreciate the value of, and power in, words, it was in this time, that I fell *in love* with words, and writing, alike; it was in this time that I realized 'No matter what I went through in life, no matter the hardships/struggles/uphill climbs I faced, I would **be okay** because I had writing in my corner.'

This is

The Chronicles of a Life Untold.

Enjoy.

Heart<u>ache</u>; Heart*break*

What am I supposed to do?

What am I supposed to do?
If I love you.
And I know you love me,
But you will not let it be.
I know we could make it,
But you don't seem to show it.
We really are perfect for each other,
But sometimes you make me feel so under the weather.
Should I just say "good-bye",
And let time fly.
Or trust my heart,
And hope it isn't broken apart.
I know the feelings I have for you are true,
But should I tell you?
Do you feel the same way?
Or is it just what I want you to say?

When....!

When I look into your eyes,
I am surprised.
That you have been hurt,
And put through so much dirt.
How do you deal with it.
Don't you just want to quit?
You try so hard,
For that one special word.
You do so much,
To be able to give that one special touch.
Do you just settle for any way,
Or does everything have to be your way?
Why do you try and be so hidden,
When you don't want to show what is within.
You are so fly,
And you wonder why I cannot say goodbye.

Goodbye to the way that you touch me,
And how you treat me.
You treat me like I'm special,
And for that I am truly gratefull
I thank you for your love,
With that I feel so above.
I thank you for you are my boo,
And I will always be with you.

<u>Broken-up</u>
What do I do if I loved you,
And I know you loved me
But it's just so hard for us to be
I mean I saw us going down-hill but I was too in denial
I didn't want to just break it off because I really did love you
But I didn't want to keep it going because I didn't know if you loved me too
It's really easy to say something when you've never experienced it
Well I guess we're over now and that's all I can say
As for you and me well I'll get over it, someday.

<u>Broken-up no.2</u>
Now that we have broken up
I really do understand
All that we could have been together
And all that I am
I know I can make it on my own
With no one tear cried at night
Because I know we did what was right
That's why I didn't put up a fight
There's no point in fighting for something that you know isn't going to work
Just suck it up and stick it with a cork
I'm not going to spread gossip around about you
Because I'm more mature than that

I just hope that you can keep that same code
And not do it back
I really am sorry about how it happened
But I know it was all for the better
Now we can both move on with our lives, live long, and prosper.

The Outsider

I'm the one who nobody cares
The one who always shares.
I'm the one who is never wanted,
I'm the one who is always taunted,
My dreams are always haunted.
I'm the one who doesn't know who she is.
The one that no one will miss.
I'm the one that puts up a front,
To hide the way I feel.
Instead of facing the world,
And trying to heal.
I Am The Outsider.

Lost Love

Stab in the chest,
Pain in the heart.
What could have been the cause,
Of this awful break apart.
Between our souls,
Between our spirit.
Something bad happened,
Beneath the turret.
I feel betrayed,
I feel hurt.
How could you treat me like this,
As if I'm just a piece of dirt.
I don't think we belong together,
But I don't know what to do.
Should I move along,
And just get over you.
Or should I stay in this relationship,
And hope it gets strong.
I'm tired of trying,
Because I feel like you're just taking this for a ride.
You are doing nothing,
If you want this relationship to work you have to do something.
But whatever we're over,
I could care less,
God, I'm so happy to finally get that off my chest.
But anyway you can finally move on now,
Like you've been wanting to do for quite some time,
I wish you the best and a happy life,
Cause I know Ima get the rest

What Would I Do?

*What would I do without your
hands around my waist.
Without your special embrace.*

*What would I do without your
sweet sweet smile.
Or how you make my life
worth while.*

*What would I do without waking
up to knowing you're were there.
Or to have someone who I know
cares.*

*What would I do without your
unique touch.
Or how you looked on that crutch.*

*What would I do without your kiss.
The one that if you were to leave I
would totally miss.
Or the way you say my name.
When I am in pain.*

*What would I do without the way
you hold me.
Or what you told me.*

*What would I do without you.
My baby boo.*

Leaving Me

A very nice day,
On our way.
How nice can it be,
To be you and me.
While, we walk,
As we talk.
You are very sweet,
My personal treat.
Why do you have to leave,
Leaving me on my knee.
How can you do this to me,
With all that we can be.
With what we are,
Me in your arms.
You are my personal favorite
So please just save it.

Hidden

Hidden is when you are under your covers,
Where nobody suffers.
Hidden is when you can't look because you're too scared,
But then again some people don't really care.
When you are scared you should have somebody to talk to,
A lot of people talk to their friends.
But I have somebody else to talk to,
I have you.

Love

Love is the feeling that you get in your stomach,
When you see that special someone.
The tingles that you feel,
When you receive your first kiss.
The way that you think of them,
When they're away.
And light up,
When they return.
Love is the little things that they do or say,
That just happen to make your day.
The way they touch you,
When you feel as little as possible.
The way they assure you everything will be ok,
Although you both know that may not be true.
Love is being held by the waist in public,
And not caring what anybody thinks or says.
Because you know you're in love,
With the one that you have.

I Remember

I remember when I was really little and so carefree,
When I was oh so dandy.
When all I had to do was go to school,
And not have to worry about being cool.
When I could dress how I wanted,
Without having to be taunted.
To play with whom I wanted to,
Without having to please you.
To be friends with who I like,
And not having it turned into a fight.
I remember when I was really little and nice,
I didn't have to worry about paying the ultimate price.

When I'm With You

When I'm with you,
I feel invincible.
As if nothing can touch me,
I'm untouchable.
The only thing I feel,
Are your arms around me.
With which I feel so protected,
But yet so free.
You are my castle and my sky,
Without you I feel so shy.
When we kiss,
My whole world lights up;
And I feel like a new born pup.
So calm and protected,
That our feelings can't be detected.
I wanna show ya' to the world,
So that everybody can know that I'm your girl.
We've only been going out for a couple of days,
But I like you in so many ways.
I like you for you are my boo,
And I will always stand beside you.
I like you as a friend,
While being with you my heart can mend.
And I like you as yourself,
Cause around you I can be myself,
And I can show my true colors,
Instead of hiding under my covers.

Your heart is my heaven,
Your eyes are my sky,
Without you it's hard to survive.

Their story; *My* Words

What Happens When it's Over?

(First):
All the happiness and joy,
But what happens when it's over?
All the kids and children toys,
But what happens when it's over?
All the hugs and kisses,
But what happens when it's over?
All the Mr. and Mrs.,
But what happens when it's over?
All the pictures and pals,
But what happens when it's over?
All the bedtime stories and lullabies,
But what happens when it's over?
All the fun and piggy back rides,
But what happens when it's over?
(Then):
All the deceiving and lies,
But what happens when it's over?
All the fights and knives,
But what happens when it's over?
All the hiding and peeking,
But what happens when it's over?
All the running around and sneaking,
But what happens when it's over?
All the pain and betrayal,
But what happens when it's over?
All the lightening and hail,
But what happens when it's over?
All the annulment papers and divorce,
But what happens when it's over?
All the hurt and force,
But what happens with it's over?
(Finally):

All the packing and moving,
But what happens when it's over?
All the roughness that you're smoothing,
But what happens when it's over?
All the custody battles and suffering children,
But what happens when it's over?
All the making angry and bewilderin',
But what happens when it's over?
What happens when it's over?
What happens when it's over?

12/2/10

Bittersweet

I love you
And I don't know why
All you ever do
Is feed my lies
We had a family
We were going strong
But then you left me
For a guy so young
I miss my daughter
She's my world
But because of your stupidity
I don't see her like I should
I loved you
Treated you right
But you went to him
Now all we do is fight
Now you're always calling me
Asking for money
Well I'm not giving it to you
Just to see your 'honey'

I hate that I still love you
That I can hardly move on
But I know I deserve to be happy
My love for you will one day be gone

Crash Course in *Reality*

The Storm and the Rain

I miss your smile
I miss your laugh
I miss the way you would sneak up behind me
And put your arms around my waist
Whenever I was with you
My heart was never at a regular pace
I miss your little brown eyes
I miss the way you would pull me into your lap
When I acted like I didn't want to kiss you
You refused to believe me and kissed me as if you'd never see me again
The way you fell asleep to me scratching your head
And loved to listen to my heart beating
My heart sunk when I heard you got hit by a car
Then I found out it wasn't true
My heart nearly split into two
I wondered why you would do that to me
Put me through that pain
Then I realized the storm never comes before the rain

1/10/09

Grandma

When you left me
I didn't know what to do
I thought my life would be over
Without you
It's been two years
Since you passed away
Although sometimes it feels
It was just yesterday
I miss your talks
I miss our laughs
I miss the way you talked to me
About your past
About your regrets
About your fears
Almost always landing us both
In tears
The way you talked to me
As if I was your child
With a voice so sweet
Tender and mild
A voice that I miss everyday
And I hope I will hear it again
Somehow, someday
But now you're up in heaven
Looking down on me
I know I can feel your presence
All around me
I miss you dearly
Always have, always will
But until I can meet you in Heaven
I will live my life to fulfill

1/14/09

Because...

Because you wrote that letter

I know how it feels to be in your arms again

Because you wrote that letter

I know how it feels to have my lips against yours

Because you wrote that letter

I have the love of my life back

Because you wrote that letter

I have never been happier

2/11/09

I Refuse

I refuse to let my child be called an "unplanned blessing"
(When) I have a child they're going to be planned and wanted
I refuse to raise a child in the economy today
An economy of money hungry, machinery based people
(When) I have a child I want them to love the outdoors, the wilderness, the natural beauty that exists
I refuse to let them grow up strictly on electronics
(When) I have a child I want them to be proud of what their parents do
(When) I have a child, they're going to have a life of travel; of adventure
I refuse to make them wish they could do more.

4/30/09

My Guardian Angel

Whenever I think about you
My eyes fill with tears
And I think back to all the years
All the good times we had together
All the great memories I still remember
All the times we laughed
All the times we cried
I wish you were still here
But I know you're looking over me and Kristina
You're my guardian angel
You keep me safe day and night
In the dark and in the light
You're always here for me to talk to
Whenever I need you
I miss you, I love you
I want to be with you
Why'd you have to leave?
You were too young to go
Now I'm here without you
And I miss you so..

September 25, 2009

Behind These Eyes

Behind these eyes
There's a lot of innocence
But there's a lot of guilt
That through the years
I have built

Behind these eyes
There's a ton of hurt
Tears that have been a river
Down my face
Washing away all my impurities
Slowly bringing out the – Truth

Behind these eyes
I hide a past
A past of regrets
Of crushed dreams
Hopeless wants
Needless pleasures

Behind these eyes
I show love
I show compassion
I show joy
I show emotion

Because of these eyes
I hide who I am
If it weren't for these eyes
I'd be in a jam.

September 25, 2009

BLEW IT!

You had your chance

You blew it

I'm happy now

Get over it

You'll never get another chance

Not with me

Now I've moved on

And I'm perfectly happy

The joy he brings to my life

Is beyond anything you could have done

I'm smiling now

Everyday

The tears are now

Gone

I hope you've moved on with your life

Cuz I sure as hell have

I finally have someone who treats me right

And my love for him is mad

9/29/09

Love and Betrayal

You were my shelter
You were my shield
Whenever He left my heart wounded
You were the doctor- who healed
When I was hurt
You led me to- your arms
When I couldn't take it
You gave me hope

When He pushed me away
You pulled me close
You showed me love
That rose above
Anything He ever showed me
Lead me to a tunnel of darkness
You brought me to the light
He made me think I was always wrong
You told me I was right
Because of you
I moved past Him
Onto you
And that same light will never get dim

March 20th- my life changed
My mind set re-arranged
Instead of being hurt
I was constantly being held
You showed me love
You showed me truth
You showed me- I can have love
Without- the hurt
Without the worry
You proved to me

Love has no hurry
You were there when I needed you
You were the tissue that wiped my tears
You were even there for me when I didn't
You comforted me- and got rid of my fears
But when I did need you
Your love was true

You've changed my life
For the better
Before you
I was repeatedly being stabbed
By a knife
I was over and over again, betrayed
But you
You came to my aid
That knife was a dagger, or
His love
Piercing my heart
-and leaving me with blood
That knife was like his love
So deep and hurt so much
My open wounds
Were your invitation
To come in and give me such..

Your kisses always passionate
Your hugs always warm
Your lips almost magical
Your arms almost home
Your ryes are my heaven
Your heart is my soul

Without you in my life baby
I don't know where I'd go
What I'd do.

10/01/09

The Problem

So I figured out the problem
It's these stupid tests and quizzes
What's it really testing?
My patience

Should I stay where I am
While everyone around me moves on
Or move with them
Without a clue of what's going on

My grades are shit
I have no potential
They won't get better
My emotions are indescribable

I don't know what I'm going to do
If I have to leave
I'll be leaving my best friend and my baby
I may as well kiss my happiness goodbye.

My mom doesn't believe that they'll go up
She's already planning on enrolling me into Options
I want to do nothing but to prove her wrong
But in reality
My grades show that I'm failing

With no way up.

I'm drowning in a pool of school
And I can't reach the surface
I can't breathe under the pressure
I'm getting smothered.

If I have to leave
I won't be able to survive
Day to day without my best friend and baby
Yeah right.

December 1, 2009

The Bitter Truth

My whole life's falling apart

I just want a new start

Everything seems to be going wrong

My feelings are getting so strong

I can hardly deny it

And I feel like shit

I can't stand seeing her hurt

She's being treated like dirt

And I can't help

It makes me want to yell

I'll never be the one who brings joy to her life

It's cutting me like a knife

But she's my best friend

Until the end

And I love her to death

Through thick and thin.

December 1, 2009

Jealousy is an Ugly Thing

So….

Ever been jealous?
It really fuckin sucks!

Especially when you're jealous of your best friend

And her relationship.

Or what she calls a relationship..

But that's not the point I'm making

My point is..

I wanna be the one to make her happy

Not any other lucky bastard…

But I'll never be so lucky

I'm just her woman..

And she's my love..

But whatever.

I'm here for her no matter what

And **NO ONE** will ever change that..

                                        EVER!!! <3

4/27/10

I'm Sorry

I'm sorry I hurt you
I'm sorry I caused you pain
But I couldn't stay with you
Knowing I didn't feel the same
To drag you along
Would have just been wrong
It would have just hurt you more
And the tears would continue to pour
The last thing I wanted
Was to be like every other girl
Who tells you how amazing you are
But then ruined your world
I know how you felt about me
And you know how I felt about you
But our levels of feelings
Just did not subdue
You really are an amazing guy
I know that for a fact
Any girl would be lucky to be yours
But I am not that one..

5/6/10

Day to Day

The way you make me feel
Doesn't seem real
That in such short time
I'm willing to put my life on the line
To save yours
Knowing that you're safe
Helps me go by
Day to day

July 23, 2010

Losing You..

I don't trust her
And I don't know why
I just have this feeling
That she's feeding him lies.
She's so damn young
In heart and in mind
He falls so easily
His past will rewind
All the heartache
All the deceiving
His heart will be broken
And there will be bleeding
Of course, I'll come in
As his best friend
And clean up the mess
From another cut open chest
All of which I've done before
But it could have been prevented
If he'd just listen to me more.

July 26, 2010

No Good

I gave her a chance

I really did

But I can't shake this feeling

I can't get it out of my head

The way she has you whipped

It's like looking at a dog at the end of its leash

It can bark and howl

But in the end it's not released.

July 28, 2010

Gone Forever

The pain won't stop

And it's not fair

I can't deny it

Because I know it's there

Everywhere I walk

Every time I breathe

I can feel it there

Like it's haunting me

A ghost that's controlling my life

It destroyed my past

And it's after my future

Like Its form of torture

All my hopes

All my dreams

Gone forever

My life, torn at the seams

10/6/10

I Love You!

How much I love him
Is beyond measures
How happy he makes me
Brings me so much pleasure
I think about him day and night
In the dark and in that light

His arms around me
Feel like home his lips against mine
Is where they belong

Everything I do
Everything I see
Is a reminder to me

Not being with him all the time is so hard to handle
But I know we have enough love

10/7/10

End of Days

Sometimes I question
The amount of love you have for me
But I don't want to
Because babe, you mean the world to me
I want to spend every waking minute with you
Never be away from you
I love you more than words can say
And I want to be with you until the
End of Days

11/15/10

Please Tell Me

Please tell me

Tell me you're missing me just as much.

Tell me that every day

You miss my touch

The way I say your name

Or the way I hold you

When you're playing the game

The way I wrap my arms around your shoulders

Because baby, you're my boulder

11/28/10

'Til The End

Lying here in bed
My eyelids heavy
Hoping I'll escape to a dream
A dream where I'll be able see you
Will be able to touch you
All day
Every day
Hear your deep voice
Feel you gentle touch
Taste you sweet kiss
And be with you
Til the end
I love you <3

11/28/10

Coming Together

My life
Is coming together
My hopes
My dreams
Ones I thought were just a dream
Finally coming within reach
My love
Better than ever
Our love
Stronger than before
His face
Brightens my darkest days
His voice
Lights my way
Our future
Becoming our reality

1/1/2011

Is This Goodbye?

What happened to you tonight?

You weren't the girl that I know

The fun, crazy, out there girl that we love

You were like a completely different person

Oblivious to what was right in front of you

All you cared about was partying

Smoking weed and getting drunk

When your girls wanted to have a fun night out with you

I saw a side of you tonight that I did not like

So tell me now, is it just a phase

Or is this goodbye?

1/1/2011

Babydoll <3

Every day that goes by

I start to like you more and more

Maybe it's your beauty

Or the way you make me smile

Maybe it's your affectionate words

Damn girl, they drive me wild

It could be your eyes

The way they light up the room

I'm not sure what it is

But baby, you make me swoon.

1/17/2011

Have I Fallen?

The way I feel about you

I don't know if I should

I think I'm falling for you

But I didn't know I could

You are so beautiful

Inside and out

Your personality is amazing

I know that without a doubt

But I feel awful

I feel pretty bad

I have a boyfriend

Who's given me all that I have

He's my heart

He's my soul

My question is,

Have I fallen for my Babydoll?

3/2/11

When Dreams Become Reality

Do you know that every day,

I fall more and more in love with you?

Every time I see you it's like the first time,

I'm nervous and the sparks fly.

Every kiss is like the first one we shared,

It leaves me breathless and wanting more.

That I dream about the day,

That I become yours, forever.

Our mischievous kids,

Doing whatever their twisted minds can come up with,

Baby, a life with you is the life for me.

March 31, 2011

I Miss You

I miss what we had.

I miss what we were.

I miss the guy you were,

Before you became who you are today.

You couldn't care less about anything or anyone,

You have no ambition, no goals; no dreams.

Where'd my best friend go?

The guy who had a hint of an idea what he wanted out of

life.

I miss him,

Not what he's become

4/11/11

& You Don't Even Try

I never thought anyone could
Make me smile
Make me laugh
Make me giggle
Give me chills
Make me want to be with them
In the same room
On the same bed
Even in their arms
As much as you do.

My desire to kiss you is
Incredible
Stronger than any feeling I've felt in so long
Deeper than the widest ocean
But lighter than a floating leaf
Just the thought of your lips against mine
Sends chills down my spine
Electricity through my body
And places images in my head

Your passion for music: for Jazz
Your unbelievable talent on guitar
Leaves me in aw, it's like nothing I've ever heard or seen
before
You get so into it
I hear beautiful music but when I look
Your fingers are barely moving
You're in your own little world
You can do so much
But with such little effort

You say the simplest things
That keep me smiling for the longest time

You understand: you listen like no one has in so long
Every minute of every day
You are on my mind
I miss you when we're not texting
I get anxious
I jump to my phone when I hear your ringtone
Or when it's on vibrate I get bummed when it's not you

When I'm lying alone in bed
I wish you were with me
Your body against mine
Your arm around me
Our fingers intertwined
Heaven on Earth

I wake up
And immediately check my phone to see if you've texted me
And when you haven't
I have to text you
I love what you say
I love how you say it
I love everything about you

When I was with you just that one day
Nothing else mattered
I had no worries
No real thoughts aside from
"How much more amazing can he be?" and…
"Goddamn, I want to kiss him."
I even found myself thinking I could
But there was just something about you that made me so damn nervous
I loved it and hated it at the same time
That day same as the day I met you,
There was just something about you that got my attention
Something that couldn't keep my eyes from wandering in your direction
Something about you that is just …
Incredible.
Amazing .
Something that attracts me to you
You're like my magnet
Every if I wanted to pull away

It'd be impossible to find the strength

You are..
What I've always wanted.
The cause of the way I've always wanted to feel

The reason for the thoughts in my head
The addition to the extra blemish on my cheeks
The hop in my step
The glow in my eyes
The smile glued to my face
You are…
Perfect.. for me, to me.
I couldn't ask for more
Or for anyone better.

August 1, 2011

I Hate Myself

I'm not who you think I am
I'll play with your heart
I'll play with your mind
I'll act so sweet
Until you're mine
Then I'll show you who I am
I'll be a bitch
I'll get feelings for someone else
And then I'll end up
Breaking your heart

August 12, 2011

Fuck My Life

It's like a disease,
Pulsing through my veins.
I can't live with it,
But it won't go away.
Every breath is a struggle,
Every day is a fight.
I try to be happy,
But this pain is so overwhelming.
I can't take it,
But I can't cry.
My fists just clench,
And my toes curl.
I hurt those I love the most,
Because of this uncertainty.

August 12, 2011

The Ugly Truth

It pulses through my body

Like a disease that I can't get rid of

It causes a struggle to live

A never-ending battle of pain

I feel it

But yet I'm numb to it

My toes curl and fists clench

But no tears can fall.

August 18, 2011

I'm Gay

No matter how hot his body,
No matter how cute his face
He just won't turn me on
Like a girl with good grace.
A beautiful smile
And piercing eyes
That's what I noticed
When you said "Hi" that first time.
You're rough around the edges
But have a kind heart.
That's what I love about you,
And have from the very start.
You stand up for what you love,
And fight for what you believe in,
You're gorgeous inside and out,
And that's what I've been seein'.
You can't fake character,
You can't hide pride,
And what I see in you,
Has caused love that will never die.

Whether you're with me,
Or some extremely lucky guy,
I'll always be here for you,
Be right by your side.
I love you now,
I love you then,
And I'll keep on loving you,
Until the very end.

October 6, 2011

Thank You

There's a weight on my shoulders,
That I can't get rid of.
A black cloud that follows me,
No matter where I go.
A fake smile,
That hides a life of despair.
A personality of happiness,
That covers a reality that's not yet prepared.
For years and years now,
All I've known is this depression.
But then you came along,
And turned it into something amazing.
The way you make me smile,
It's real.. It's genuine.
How easily you make me laugh,
Makes me feel like a kid again.
There's something about your warm eyes,
And kind heart,

That when I look at you,
I practically melt.

I lie in your arms,
And everything's alright.
I kiss you on the lips,
And I want to stay with you all night.
You have taken my heart,
And held it so securely.
And when I ask you "Why me?",
"Why would you deal with my back?"
You tell me, "Because I know you."
"You're easily the most beautiful girl I've ever met, I love your personality.
And this is just physical, it's not you, it's just what's happening to you."
You have no idea what it means to me,
To find love with all that's going on with my body.

Life *Happens*; Keep <u>Going</u>

Don't Let Your Pride Consume You

All the times I stood up for you,
told you that you deserved better.
I had a feeling things would change,
once you got a year older.

The light in your eyes grew dimmer
and the passion in your heart became weaker.
As much as I tried to keep you from that,
I was no match for the partying and liquor.

I was the best friend I could be for you,
helping you through tough times and struggles.
But I guess my efforts weren't enough,
so now my friendship will become idle.

You will be missed, but not so much mourned.
Because I have a strange feeling once you're without me for some time,
a lesson you will have learned.

That I'm a truly great friend,
always there through thick and thin.
You may not think so now,
but you will be back in the end.

2/13/13

Be the Change!

Open your ears and close your mouth
I've got somethin' to talk to y'all about
There's so much hate
So much controversy
But where'd it all start
Can someone please tell me?

You point fingers so fast and carefree
But by doing that what's it helping any?
What makes you so much better than the next
What makes you feel the need to put them to the test
There's nothing wrong with love and forgiveness
It's a hellofalot better than roughin' someone up over a drama fest.

When it comes to life
Nobody's perfect
We live and learn
And sometimes kick the bucket
We've all broken promises
We should have kept
We've all done things
We shouldn't have
There's no way of knowing
Who's wrong or right
So why bother
Puttin' up a fight
Accept your mistakes
Strive to be better
And one day this world
May not be so bitter

There's still hope
For future generations
If we can only suck up our pride
And get the motors runnin'
Talk is cheap
Actions speak
Words can be changed
But actions create a name!

12/15/14

What good is it to be different, if it just brings people pain?

What good is it to be intelligent, if there's no one to understand?

What good is it to be kind, in a world ridden with hate?

What good is it to think before you speak, when everyone speaks through pained emotions and cruel words?

What good is it to be me, when the world can't handle it?

5/21/15

Monologue

And she said to herself "Why is it people only see my body?"

And she said to her "Because beauty and brains is unheard of, my dear."

She replied "But my beauty IS my brains."

She sighed and replied "Darling, the world is too jaded to see that."

5/21/15

Prisoner

I am a prisoner at war
a war of my own mind
a war of my own body
a war that I can't win
a war that's seeing causalities of sanity

5/21/15

Happiness Eluding

And that's when my happiness disappeared
As if it were surgically removed
Scraped off by a scalpel
Only to leave a mouth hole

5/21/15

We live in a time where
When we have an issue with someone
Instead of talking it out with them
We post a vague status on Facebook
We want numbers
in follows and friends
but don't even know how
to be a friend
we no longer
do something out of the kindness
of our own hearts
we need some sort of payment
we live behind a mask of anonymity
blinded by the mist of comfort
we'd rather know what a remote stranger
is saying about us
than ask how our closest friend
is doing
...
Everything is
Text, tweet, post
Everything is so
Impersonal
But we wonder why

We don't have deeper connections with people
It's because we don't
Even have a deep connection
To ourselves, our true selves

5/21/15

All I'm doing is lying here thinking
But I'm not actually thinking
It's like a black hole of things
Around the edges
But nothing in the middle to make
Sense of the madness
There's something on my mind
In my mind
But it's not on my tongue
Not something my fingers can quite find
It's seeking
Desperately searching
In the dark
Almost lurking
It's like I can feel it working
Working working
But the pages are blank
All the effort is there
The effect though, is —

11/19/15

Dysphoria

When you're staring into an abyss
And you can't find bliss
You know something's wrong
And you can't go on
With the way things are
They're gone too far
And the way things are going
You can't help but have them showing
Which makes you feel scared and afraid
And that makes you feel ashamed
You are trapped and lost
And just looking for a change
                      At any cost.

Lay Down To Rest

People say she's the strongest girl they know,

That's just because she puts on a show.

Truth is, behind the painted on smile and upbeat personality,

Lives a girl who just wants to end this misery.

Day to day it seems as though her life just gets worse,

When will someone lift this wicked curse?

All she wants is to be happy,

But day in and day out all she's feeling is crappy.

Depression follows her like a black cloud over her head,

Sometimes she thinks she'd be better off dead.

At least then there'd be no more stress,

She could finally lay down to rest.

11/17/2015

Not a Warrior

I really don't know how much longer I can keep this up

I feel so weak

Yet everyone insists that I'm so strong

Like a warrior

Only I'm fighting a battle that'll never truly be won

A battle with my own mind

My own body

A battle against what I can't stop from happening

And the little that I can do to help ease the pain that's deafening

I want to scream

I want to cry

But my vocals won't budge

And my eyes won't shed

I'm tired of being sick

I'm tired of being tired

I'm exhausted of being sick and tired

Drained every moment of every day

Able to gather just 'enough' to get things out of the way

No more "what I want"

No more options

Only "what I need"

And demands

11/17/2015

Strong

I feel the walls,
They're caving in
I keep trying to fight
But feel like I'll never really win
Some days are better than other
Some days really fucking suck
I feel like I'm out in the middle of nowhere
A sitting duck
Waiting for my next ailment to make its mark
And BOOM,
It gets even harder.
I want to be social
I want to have friends
But this pain
It just never ever ends
And I try to resist
The wretched curse of drugs and alcohol
And while I've succeeded so far
Some days it seems impossible

I just want one little sip

To dull the pain

One little pill

To drift away

But I can't do that

No I can't

I have to stay strong

Even if 'strong' is the last thing I feel.

12/14/15

Just a Room

Nobody knows

The battle that I go through

On a daily basis

A prisoner of my own body

My spirit wants to be free

But I can't let go

Because my body owns me

Even those who know

Don't truly understand

Every day is a fight

Will I or will I not survive

Can I hold on much longer

Or will I just end it tonight

A pill too much

But even then no luck

High immunity

Inevitable migraine

But no relief

From the real pain

From the question that haunts me every day

Will I ever see an end to this doom

Or will I be forever confined

To just a room

1/27/16

She wanted to be seen
As something besides beautiful
For more than her looks
But she knew
The unfortunate reality
That if she wasn't a Beauty
She'd become Invisible

1/28/16

I Was Beautiful

I was beautiful.
Bright blue eyes
Long blonde hair
Thin but curvy frame

I was beautiful
Captivating smile
Infectious laugh
Flawless features

I was beautiful
Constant compliments
Heads turned
Eyes stared

I was beautiful
Beauty was me
I was not my mind
I was not my heart
I was not my soul

I was beautiful
No hopes
No dreams
No desires

I was beautiful
A specimen to be looked upon

A 'sight to see'
Expected to enjoy the attention

I was beautiful
Every unwelcomed advance
Every daunting glance
Every misguided attempt at conversation

I was beautiful
So nobody cared what else I was
It was a shock that I was caring
Unreal that I was open-minded
People fell for me because I was 'different'

Beauty is expectation
Beauty is responsibility
Beauty is not being able to be anything more

I was beautiful
Beauty owned me
I was beautiful
But nobody saw me.
I was only beautiful.

6/18/16

Beauty

is a monster

wrapped

in a pretty package

of desire

12/11/16

The Drones

Our electronics have more
emotions than we do

Our Facebook page has more
friends than we know

Our Twitter has more
Followers than friends

Our Snapchat has more
10 second stories than lifelong histories

Our Instagram has more
Heart than we give each other

We've become our own paparazzi
With the same lack of dept
Our devices see more of us
Than we see of ourselves

In a time of technology and
Human interaction

We have become
The Drones

12/21/16

Society

We blame society

We are society

We are to blame

We take no responsibility

Giving Way to Reality

It's not always a matter of
giving up or giving in
But accepting that there are some fights in life
you just can't win
So I'll count my losses
and take what's left
Look towards tomorrow
and hope it all works out for the best

When It Rains, It Pours

Here it comes

in waves

until

it floods

Thoughts

fears

emotions

tears

All at once

then nothing at all

I don't know

what to do

I haven't an idea

who to call

Just stuck

in this thing-

Called reality
can't help thinking
it's nothing but
A fallacy

1/9/17

Pretty Girl

Because no one wants to

 feel bad for the pretty girl.

She's got it all.

The looks

The attention

The admiration

The love

Trouble is,

 She doesn't have

The freedom

She; Not Me

I was Her
But She was
Not Me
While everyone saw
A Beauty Queen
I saw Beauty
But I did not
See me.

The *Realities* of **Thought**

Our brains are truly unique, they are the most unique of everything we have, everything we are. Our brain is the one thing that makes us an individual, its unlimited potential and growth, constant expansion and evolvement; it sculpts us, to who we are based on our experiences, every experience alters our perception and perspective. It, alone, is the essence of our being.

Unfortunately, because the brain is ever evolving, changing and interpreting, we can never get a full grasp of our reality, so we live in a fantasy of thoughts and ideas, beliefs and theories. We don't know who we are, so we seek to fit into what we think we can be. The irony of this being, as undeniably unique and an individual that we are, we find comfort in being a part of something, in settling for what is obviously a clique. As much as we say we don't want to fit in, we don't care what other's think, our constant repetition of successful camouflages and endless seeking for meaning, proves entirely different.

The tragedy in all this is, we try so hard to be different, but the one thing that makes us truly unique, our mind, is the same thing that is grossly wasted.

"Why flaunt a hot body
when you can flaunt a beautiful mind?"
Because everyone understands <u>sex appeal</u>;
not everyone comprehends **intelligence**.

It's called Self Expression; not Self Definition.

Everything we are is only a part of who we are, it does not;
it should not, define us 5.21.15

Definition to make sense of what the heart feels is like a
circle, there is no point. 9.4.14

I used to think I'd rather be admired than anything, but now I've come to learn that even admiration is only surface deep when there's no real understanding 9/4/14

Personality should never come at the cost of character

Simplicity in possession; complexity in mind 9.4.14

Context and intent must always matter; perception and perspective are vital to the human experience.

Be smart, but be open. Don't be afraid to make those mistakes because that's how you're going to learn 9/4/14

I remember, as kids growing up, if we fell, we got back up and tried it again, once the same way to see if the first time was a fluke, and then differently until we got it right. We learned; we adapted. While we felt momentary pain, we overcame it through using it to learn. Pain is a teacher; Life is a lesson- Learn.

Unity doesn't have to be similarities; but a love for differences

The more you know yourself, the better you can understand others. 9.4.14

Obey the boundaries without being bound by them 9.4.14

Maybe one day we'll get bored of comparing opposites and we'll learn to love the beauty in difference they each have. 5.21.15

Why can't we enjoy each other's company without it having to mean something else, lead to something or be anything other than two people enjoying each other's company? 5.21.15

I like talking about things that matter. Things that can change, alter or affect me; not things that allow me to come out the same person as I was going into the conversation 5.21.15

Desperate times call for desperate measures
Desperate hearts call for desperate pleasures
Desperate minds call for desperate saviors 9.4.14

The only time there's not more to the story is when the book is over and there are no more, but even then, we sometimes let our imaginations run wild. In real life, there's always more to the story, unfortunately the thing we let run wild isn't so innocent, rather, it's assumption and judgement. 5.21.15

Being alive does not mean living
For living is to experience
To experience is to be open
To be open is to live
To live is to be alive
5.21.15

A true friend will tell you what you **need** to hear, even if it's not what you *want* to hear.

Life isn't hard
Life isn't easy
Life isn't fair
Or unfair
Life is life
The simplest way to put it
It is what it is
But that doesn't have to be all it is 5.21.15

I am sick
My body is my sickness
There is no known cure
Or real relief
Just a believe that I am meant
To change the world

The way my sickness changed me
5.21.15

We post everything on social media; yet most of us don't even have social lives 5.21.15

We're more likely to forget our wallet than our phone; our wallet **holds** our identity, our phone *is* our identity 5.21.15

Confidence is humble, not boastful
It doesn't brag
Or belittle
It's heartfelt
And helpful
Because it knows
It remembers what it was like
To not be so

What you have and what you want;
What you seek and what you find;
What you need and what you get

We share everything with everyone; we don't share anything with anyone.

Like a bird that's lost its flight; a candle that's lost its light

We're so afraid of being alone mentally and emotionally, that we're desperate to surround ourselves with people who leave us alone physically

It's amazing how you know yourself best when you're young, then you grow up and try to find yourself due to superficial ideas

How do you want to be remembered, for your honor or your pride?
How do you want to be remembered, for your body or your mind?

To know so much, but understand so little

When you truly don't care what others think, you do what makes your heart happy; that makes you shine.

We no longer care what others see in us, we're so
desperate for attention that we'll accept the shallowest of
attraction so long as it suits our desires

I like knowing what people are thinking when they say
things because while actions speak louder than words,
thoughts speak louder than actions

I'm feeling restless in this body that doesn't feel like mine
A soul that's still searching
A heart that's desperately wanting
A mind that's always wandering

You can't control how others act,
But you can control how you react;

Don't let others' actions
Dictate your reactions

Love is the greatest weapon of all. Why?
Because it doesn't need to be threatening or violent, to be powerful.

You are worth more than what you are worth to others

You're a dream; I never thought I'd have because I always thought my reality overruled my imagination

I'm fighting:
My entire body and my mind being my illness, sickness, disease, cage and life sentence.

"If it's not one thing, it's another. If it helps one thing, it makes another worse."

"I don't remember who I was without pain. I don't remember a day before pain. And I don't remember what it's like to not be in pain every second of every day."

10.21.15

We're creatures of habit
Only they run so rampant
That we cannot control them
So we cannot contain them
And then
We lose sight of who we are

My body is beat
My soul is aching
My heart is crying
My mind is numbed

10.24.15

There comes a time when you can't help but wonder if it's
the little things that shape you, rather than the big things
that impact you 11.1.15

Even from the darkest of places
Beauty can show
It just has to be nourished with love and patience
To be able to grow

We are all branches of the same tree
All connected to little leaves
Some fall to the ground
For others blossom and bloom
But comparing yourself
To the growth next to you
Will only keep you from
Having the success that you can, too
11.6.15

The best way to become who you're meant to be is to cease comparing yourself to others

11.10.15

Sexiness isn't so much in how you look or how you dress, but in how you act and how you express yourself.

If the ease of things was taken out of things being done, I wonder who would still do it.

About the Author

Lee Slone is a Small Business Owner with an online shop, where she sells things she makes by hand. She is a natural born Writer who has an immense passion for words and their power of emotion; she has been writing her entire life; has a gift for words and an uncanny ability to portray, through words, what many can't articulate themselves. She has the utmost love, appreciation and respect for words; to her, they give life, they live, and they are alive.

When she's not working on things to sell for her Shop, she enjoys casually reading, watching shows on Netflix, playing with her cat, spending time with her mom/family, and habitually, but passionately, writing whatever comes to mind. When asked what she writes about, her common answer is "Whatever comes to mind. I started with poetry at a young age as a way to express myself and get things out in a private manner, as I got older, I branched out into writing songs, raps, parodies, quotes; manuscripts. I just write, and it takes whatever form it may." As well as this book, she has a couple other manuscripts underway, at least one of which, she hopes to have published one day.

She has a strong belief in the therapeutic benefits of writing and will diligently testify to the fact that it's saved her on multiple occasions. Whenever she's turned to for advice, the first thing she does is listen to what the person is saying, ask them how they're feeling, and advise them to 'Write it out.', that even if it's not coherent , or legible, the energy of thought- to-pen-to-paper will help them release whatever they're feeling at that moment; that while it may not make everything better, it'll certainly help- and that in writing, you're giving yourself a personal record to reflect on, grow from and have as a reminder of where you've been, where you are, and where you're going; that the possibilities, and benefits, of writing are endless.

She is physically disabled and quite limited, but ambitious and determined to leave a mark on this world. She refuses to become a victim of her circumstances; while she must abide by some limitations, she never stops growing. She believes that as hard as life gets, over all, it's what you make of it- So she does her best to make hers great.

Made in the USA
Middletown, DE
24 February 2017